# KING!

## THE SPORTS CAREER OF BILLIE JEAN KING

BY:

# JAMES & LYNN HAHN

EDITED BY:

# DR. HOWARD SCHROEDER

Professor in Reading and Language Arts
Dept. of Elementary Education
Mankato State University

## CRESTWOOD HOUSE

Mankato, Minnesota

# CIP

**LIBRARY OF CONGRESS CATALOGING IN PUBLICATION DATA**

Hahn, James.
   King! The sports career of Billie Jean King.

   (Sports legends)
   SUMMARY: A biography of Billie Jean King, a United States women's tennis champion, whose work to help women gain equality in tennis has completely changed the women's game into an important pro sport.
   1. King, Billie Jean — Juvenile literature. 2. Tennis players — United States — Biography — Juvenile literature. [1. King, Billie Jean. 2. Tennis players] I. Hahn, Lynn. II. Schroeder, Howard. III. Title. IV. Series.
GV994.K56H33       796.342'092'4    [B]   [92]     81-9822
ISBN 0-89686-134-1 (lib. bdg.)                     AACR2
ISBN 0-89686-149-4 (pbk.)

     **INTERNATIONAL STANDARD**
     **BOOK NUMBERS:**
     0-89686-134-1 Library Bound
     0-89686-149-4 Paperback

     **LIBRARY OF CONGRESS**
     **CATALOG CARD NUMBER:**
     81-9822
     AACR2

# PHOTO CREDITS:

Cover: Focus on Sports, Inc.

Wide World Photos: 3, 5, 11 (left), 20-21, 39, 46
United Press International: 6, 9, 14, 15, 19, 22, 25
      28, 29, 32, 35, 36, 38, 41, 43, 44
Harper & Row Publishers: 11 (right)
Courtesy Mrs. Clyde Walker: 13
Courtesy Los Angeles Tennis Club: 17

## CRESTWOOD HOUSE

Crestwood House, Inc., Box 3427, Hwy. 66 So., Mankato, MN 56001

# KING!

# CHAPTER 1

Billie Jean King is more than a tennis legend!

Sure, she won the Wimbledon singles title six times, the United States Open singles championship four times, and hundreds of other tennis tournaments. In fact, few tennis players, men or women, have won as many titles as Billie Jean King.

But, Billie Jean King gave tennis more than great play. She was the first to prove that women are a vital part of pro sports. The way Billie Jean played tennis showed fans that women's tennis was just as thrilling as men's.

Billie Jean was the first to demand and earn equal prize money for women. That wasn't easy to do. Billie Jean spent many hours talking about her plans. She argued with some of the leaders in tennis. She started the first women's tennis tour in the United States. Finally, she formed the Women's Tennis Association (WTA).

Women's tennis is popular and fun now, thanks to Billie Jean King. Without her work, some women would not have been able to enjoy tennis success.

The woman who gave the most to tennis began her life in Long Beach, California. Billie Jean was born there on November 22, 1943. She was

Billie Jean poses with the three Wimbledon trophies she won in 1973. She won the Women's Singles and Doubles, as well as the Mixed Doubles championships. She had done the same thing in 1967.

named for her father, William J. Moffitt.

"We, of course, didn't know if the first child was going to be a boy or a girl," Mr. Moffitt said. "But, her mother, Betty, knew it was going to be a Bill."

Billie Jean's father was a fireman for the Long Beach Fire Department. When Billie Jean was two, she had fun sliding down the pole at the firehouse with her father. "I remember this cat," Billie Jean related. "She'd slide down the pole all by herself!"

When she was young, Billie Jean's father started to teach her about sports. Her father began playing catch with her with a baseball when she was four.

Although Billie Jean's parents weren't poor, there were things they couldn't afford. Her father didn't have the extra money to buy his daughter a baseball bat. So, he carved one from an old piece of wood.

"I thought that was the greatest thing in the world!" Billie Jean said. "I tried to hit the ball with that homemade bat. He'd pitch to me by the hour. I didn't do too badly."

When Billie Jean was in kindergarten, she did something unusual for a girl her age. She started thinking about her future. "I felt I was going to do something special with my life," she said. "I really wanted to make my mark in the world!"

Billie Jean began to make her mark at Los Cerritos Elementary School. Learning to read and write was fun for Billie Jean. However, she had most of her fun after school.

"I loved to play football," Billie Jean said. "I always wanted to carry the ball."

Because her father was a fireman, Billie Jean was made an honorary chief by the Philadelphia Fire Department in 1973.

Billie Jean never lost her interest in softball. She was a co-founder of the Women's Professional Softball Association. Here she throws out the first ball in a 1976 game.

Basketball, softball and running were some of Billie Jean's favorite sports. Many nights after supper, her dad timed the neighborhood children in a race down the block. Most of the time, Billie Jean won.

As a fourth grader, Billie Jean liked looking at the maps in her classroom. "I'd pick out cities and dream about visiting them someday," she said. "I wanted to know what the people were like in other cities. I wanted to find out if the kids were different from my friends in Long Beach."

When Billie Jean was ten years old, she played for the Houghton Park girls' softball team. Although most of the other girls were teenagers, Billie Jean was the starting shortstop. Her fine catches and throws helped the team win the city title.

Although Billie Jean was relaxed when playing sports, she was shy in the classroom. When she was in fifth grade, she had a big problem. She had to give an oral book report in front of her class. Hitting baseballs didn't scare Billie Jean, but talking in front of the whole class did.

When the teacher asked her to give the book report, Billie Jean said she wasn't ready. Finally, her teacher sent a note home to her parents. The note said Billie Jean would fail if she didn't give the report.

When Billie Jean's father read the note, he became very upset. "No daughter of mine is going to fail a class!" he shouted.

"Dad, I can't do it," Billie Jean cried. "I get nervous and I'm scared to death."

Many years later, Billie Jean told writers what else happened that night. "My father spanked me," she said. "And that was the lesson for the night. There were certain things you had to do."

The next day was one of Billie Jean's roughest. "When the teacher called on me, I thought I was going to pass out," she said. "I stood up and stuttered, 'This book is about . . .' Then my whole body turned to jelly."

Billie Jean had to struggle to finish the book report. Although she didn't do a good job, she passed the course.

Billie Jean continued to have problems giving oral reports in the sixth grade. To help her, a teacher advised Billie Jean to talk about subjects she liked. The teacher suggested Billie Jean talk about baseball.

When Billie Jean gave an oral report about baseball, she learned something important. "I found out other kids were interested in what I was saying," Billie Jean said, "because I was, too. I saw they were listening. After baseball I talked about blimps. After that, my oral reports were okay."

When Billie Jean was only ten years old, she had begun to plan for a job. She wanted a career as a baseball player. One night during supper her dad told her women couldn't make a living in baseball. He suggested that Billie Jean think about a tennis career.

The next day she wanted to start playing tennis, but she didn't have a racket. So, she began washing neighbors' windows to earn money. She put all the money she earned into a glass jar in the kitchen cupboard.

When the jar had eight dollars in it, Billie Jean and her parents went downtown. Billie Jean chose a tennis racket with a maroon handle and nylon strings. Then, she headed straight for the tennis courts.

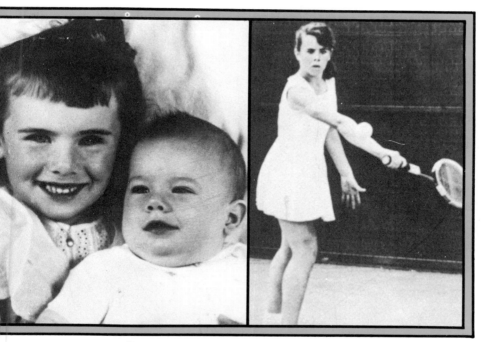

A young Billie Jean holds her brother Randy (left), and shows her early tennis form.

"You can believe this or not," Billie Jean told writers years later, "but that first day I really fell in love with tennis. I began with that eight-dollar racket and some old tennis balls on a public court. Right away I felt tennis was going to be my sport."

Billie Jean hit tennis balls that first day for a couple of hours. "I was having so much fun," she said. "I felt like I was in another world. The first time I hit a tennis ball I knew what I wanted. I wanted a career in tennis."

The second time Billie Jean played tennis was the day she had her first tennis lesson. Many years later she still remembered everything about that day. "It was at Houghton Park in Long Beach," she said. "It was a Tuesday in September and I wasn't quite eleven years old. I can still see how perfectly blue the sky was that day. I can still see the eucalyptus trees and those two cement courts."

Clyde Walker was Billie Jean's tennis teacher. He gave inexpensive tennis lessons at the city's public tennis courts. The first thing he taught her was how to hold the racket correctly. Then he taught her how to hit the ball correctly.

After Clyde showed Billie Jean how to hit a tennis ball, he told her to try it. "I dropped the ball," she said, "and swung, and hit it. It even went over the net!"

After her tennis lesson, Billie Jean's mother picked her up and asked how it went.

Clyde Walker points out some details to Billie Jean and Jerry Cromwell, another young pupil.

"Great," Billie Jean said, "just great! I want to play tennis forever. I'm going to be the best tennis player in the whole world."

"That's fine, dear," Billie Jean's mother said. She thought Billie Jean would soon get tired of tennis. She didn't think her daughter had a chance to be the best player in the world.

Within a few days, Billie Jean was really hooked on tennis. School was out at 3:10 in the afternoon. "By three o'clock," Billie Jean said, "I was so excited I could hardly stand it. I was almost halfway to the tennis courts by the time the bell stopped ringing."

Billie Jean learned by studying all-time greats, Pancho Gonzales (left) and Maureen "Little Mo" Connolly.

Every night after supper, Billie Jean practiced against an old wooden fence next to her house. She hit so many tennis balls into it she wrecked it. Her dad had to build a new fence with cement blocks.

Before bedtime, Billie Jean read books about tennis legends. She enjoyed the stories of such all-time greats as Maureen Connolly and Tony Trabert.

Billie Jean even saw a few tennis legends play in person. "I used to watch Pancho Gonzales and Lew Hoad play in Los Angeles," she said. "Watching them made me play better. It helped me keep on trying to improve."

# CHAPTER 2

Billie Jean didn't become a tennis star overnight. She played her first tournament three months after her first lesson. A friend from school beat her in the finals, 6-0, 6-0.

That first loss surprised Billie Jean. "I had blisters all over my feet!" she said. "I learned that tennis wasn't all fun. I found out it was going to be a lot of hard work."

Billie Jean wanted to win, so she decided to work harder. She began getting up at 5:30 every morning to exercise and jump rope. She practiced tennis whenever she had a chance.

In her next tournament, Billie Jean played a nineteen-year-old. Although the girl was much older, Billie Jean won the match, 6-3, 6-4.

After that win, Billie Jean asked her parents if she could play in more events. It cost a lot of money to travel to tournaments, but her parents agreed to help her. "My dad got by on only two pairs of shoes for several years," Billie Jean said. "My mother sold household products door-to-door to bring in extra money."

By the time Billie Jean was fourteen, she was playing junior tennis very well. In 1958, she won

Southern California's junior tennis title.

Billie Jean now began dreaming about Wimbledon, the most famous tennis tournament in the world. She dreamed about playing on the grass courts surrounded by ivy-colored walls. "I even picked Wimbledon as the topic for an essay I wrote," she said. The essay was about her dreams of playing and winning Wimbledon.

Billie Jean was willing to give things up to get to Wimbledon. Many times she said she couldn't go on dates or to slumber parties with her friends. Instead she practiced, practiced, and practiced. "I

This is the Los Angeles Tennis Club, where Billie Jean played for the Southern California junior tennis title.

missed a great deal," she said years later. "Some kids thought I was an oddball."

All the hours of practice began paying off for Billie Jean when she was fifteen. She was playing well and was ranked number five in the United States in the Girls 15-and-Under bracket.

Since Billie Jean played so well, tournament officials invited her to play in the Eastern United States in some grass court tournaments. She was one step closer to Wimbledon. At the time Wimbledon officials invited American women who played well on grass courts, the type of courts at Wimbledon.

Although Billie Jean played well in the East, she didn't win as many matches as she wanted. One problem was she ate too much ice cream and candy, and gained twenty pounds. To lose weight that fall, Billie Jean walked the four miles to school each day.

In 1959, a sporting goods business helped Billie Jean take lessons from Alice Marble. Alice Marble was a tennis legend from the 1930's and 1940's. Billie Jean stayed with Alice on weekends. Alice taught her some advanced shot-making skills. "She also taught me what it was like to be a champion," Billie Jean said. "She told me how Don Budge, Bobby Riggs, Helen Hull Jacobs, Helen Wills Moody, and other great players won titles. All Alice's talk rubbed off on me. It gave me an idea of what it

**Alice Marble is shown on her way to winning the 1939 Wimbledon title.**

These are the courts at Wimbledon that Billie Jean dreamed about.

would be like for me when the time came."

Billie Jean was hooked on tennis. "I had to lock her in her room at night," Alice Marble said, "to make her study."

In 1960, Billie Jean played her way into the finals of the National Girls 18-and-Under Championship. However, she lost to Karen Hantze in the final. Instead of feeling sorry for herself, Billie Jean worked more hours.

In the spring of 1961, when Billie Jean was a

senior in high school, one of her dreams came true. She received an invitation to play at Wimbledon.

Two days before graduation day at Long Beach High School, Billie Jean left for England.

Life in England wasn't like Billie Jean's dreams. At first, her hostess didn't treat Billie Jean kindly. Since Billie Jean was a newcomer at Wimbledon, she had to earn respect. Her hostess gave her just a roll and a glass of milk for breakfast. Billie Jean had to wash her dirty tennis clothes every night.

After Billie Jean won a match, she got a bigger breakfast. She was served a roll, a glass of milk, and a glass of orange juice. After she won another match, her hostess added one piece of bacon. As Billie Jean proved she deserved to play at Wimbledon, she received better treatment.

Billie Jean didn't win any more singles matches at Wimbledon that year. However, she and Karen Hantze won the women's doubles title. These two American teens were the youngest ever to win the doubles trophy. Although they weren't picked to

Karen Hantze and Billie Jean proudly show their 1961 Wimbledon Doubles trophy.

win, Billie Jean and Karen were the best doubles team in the world. In the final, Billie Jean's strong backhands helped defeat Margaret Smith and Jan Lehane, 6-3, 6-4.

# CHAPTER 3

Billie Jean was playing skillful tennis. However, she still wasn't sure she could make a living playing tennis. She had learned a lot but knew that playing professional tennis was hard work. At the time, even the best women players could not make a living playing tennis. There just wasn't enough prize money for the women. Billie Jean feared that if she played tennis full-time, she'd never earn enough money to pay her bills.

So, in the fall of 1961, Billie Jean went to Los Angeles State College. She planned on getting a college degree so she could get a job that would pay her tennis expenses. "I met a lot of new people in college," she said. "I just loved to sit around and talk."

In 1962, Wimbledon officials invited Billie Jean back to the tournament. There, she shocked thousands of tennis fans. She defeated Margaret Smith, a great singles champion, in the second round.

However, Billie Jean lost in the quarter-finals.

Billie Jean knew if she worked harder, she'd improve. She put in hundreds of hours on the tennis courts in 1962.

The next year Billie Jean surprised the tennis world at Wimbledon again. The nineteen-year-old won her way into the finals.

She faced Margaret Smith again. This time, though, Billie Jean lost. "When I walked off the court," Billie Jean said, "I felt like a real failure. It wasn't a good feeling. I didn't want to have that feeling ever again."

In 1964, Billie Jean had that bitter feeling of failure again. She lost in the semi-finals at Wimbledon. However, she didn't throw in the towel. Billie Jean tried to find out why she couldn't win at Wimbledon.

Finally, Billie Jean decided she had to change the way she played tennis. In October, 1964, she decided she could improve only if she played tennis full-time. She quit college and went to Australia. There, she took lessons from Mervyn Rose. He was one of the best tennis teachers in the world.

Mervyn Rose made Billie Jean play tennis for eight hours a day. He changed her serve and forehand. Billie Jean spent hundreds of hours trying to put more slice into her serve and more topspin on her forehand.

At first, the changes in her game caused Billie

Billie Jean serves to Margaret Smith in their 1963 match at Wimbledon.

Jean some problems. In one match she double-faulted thirty-five times with her new serve. Some people told her to go back to the old style. However, Billie Jean stuck with the new serve and it finally improved her tennis.

Early in 1965, Billie Jean flew back to the United States. With her new game, she didn't lose any matches in American tournaments.

However, Billie Jean still didn't win Wimbledon in 1965. Then, in the finals of the 1965 United States Open, Billie Jean lost to her old rival, Margaret Smith. After that loss, she vowed to put in more hours on the practice courts than ever before.

Billie Jean took time out from practice, in September, 1965, to marry Larry King, her college sweetheart.

**Billie Jean married Larry King on September 17, 1965.**

26

1966 was the year all Billie Jean's time and effort paid off. However, during the 1966 Wimbledon final against Maria Bueno, Billie Jean felt nervous and edgy. "I couldn't get rid of my tension and relax," she said. "I felt I was near the goal I'd been working toward for most of my life. I didn't want anything to stop me from reaching it."

Billie Jean overcame tension by telling herself she couldn't let it keep her from her goal. She stopped feeling nervous when she thought of all the hours she had practiced. In a great match, 6-3, 3-6, 6-1, Billie Jean won Wimbledon's women's singles title. Finally, she had won the most important tennis title in the world.

That year Billie Jean also won the U.S. Hardcourt event, the South African singles title, and the U.S. Indoors tournament.

In 1967, Billie Jean won more tennis titles. She won Wimbledon, the U.S. Indoors, and the South African titles again. Then she won the most important tennis title in the United States — the U.S. Open.

After the 1967 tennis season, Billie Jean King was ranked the Number One women's tennis player in the world.

Billie Jean had done all she could as an amateur. Now she wanted to make her living playing tennis. On April 1, 1968, she signed a contract for $40,000 per year to play with the National Tennis League in Europe. "I couldn't have been happier," she said. "At last I was a pro tennis player — something I'd wanted to be most of my life."

Billie Jean began her life as a tennis pro in Paris, France. After Paris, she played in Cannes, Nice, and in several other cities throughout Europe.

Playing tennis in all those romantic cities sounds like fun. "It was hard work," Billie Jean said. "The whole tour was nothing but one-night stands. I was never so tired in my life."

Billie Jean finished most of her matches at two in the morning. Usually, she didn't fall asleep until four. Then, she had to get up at six to be at the airport at seven. "We often had to catch a plane at eight o'clock," she said.

After the plane landed, Billie Jean boarded a bus for the long ride to the site of the tennis matches.

Laughter helped Billie Jean and the other women adjust to their tough schedules. "There wasn't must else to do besides laugh," she said. "In one place the showers didn't work. In another, the locker room was covered with cobwebs."

Billie Jean played well on tour until she hurt her left knee. "I was in almost constant pain," she said. "I took six hot baths a day to ease the pain. It was the wrong thing to do. I should've been putting ice on my knee. But, I didn't know that."

Despite the pain, Billie Jean won the women's

**Billie Jean beat Judy Tegart of Australia to win the 1968 Wimbledon crown.**

Wimbledon singles title for the third straight year. "I have to admit I never should have," she said. "I was tired and my knee really hurt."

Finally, Billie Jean couldn't stand the pain any longer. In October, 1968, she had knee surgery. Then, it took her six months of weight lifting and jogging to make the knee strong again.

Those six months weren't easy ones for Billie Jean. "I hated to lift weights," she said, "even though I know it helped my knee. Jogging for the sake of jogging bored me to tears. I loved to stay up late although I knew I needed my sleep. I went crazy around candy bars and ice cream, but I knew they caused me weight problems."

# CHAPTER 4

1969 wasn't a good year for Billie Jean. She won just one major tennis title — the South African singles.

Billie Jean began playing well again in 1970. She won the Italian singles title. Then she hurt her right knee. In July, she had another operation. "I almost looked forward to the surgery," she said. Although she knew she would hate the recovery time, Billie Jean also knew the surgery would stop the pain and help her play tennis again.

"Everything in the hospital went well," Billie Jean said after the operation. "I was out playing again within two months. I even won a couple of tournaments within four months."

Although Billie Jean had won two tennis titles after her operation, she was not happy with the sport. She felt that women tennis players weren't being treated fairly. The United States Lawn Tennis Association (USLTA) paid men more money than women for the same events. Also, the men had fifteen more tournaments than the women.

By 1970, after much work, Billie Jean and other women pros decided to form their own tennis tour, independent of the USLTA. They began with an event in Houston, Texas. It was very successful! Thousands of fans paid to see the women play. That surprised many male tennis officials. It proved women's tennis was exciting enough to attract large crowds and deserve big prize money.

In October, November, and December, Billie

Many of the top women pros defied the USLTA and formed their own tour in 1970. Billie Jean is fourth from the right.

Jean planned the women's tour for 1971. She talked with sponsors and arranged for tournament sites. She even hired umpires and ball girls. During the winter of 1971, Billie Jean played in thirteen of the fourteen women's tour matches. She won eight.

The 1971 tennis season was going great for Billie Jean until the United States Open. Then, just before her semi-final match against Chris Evert, her nerves upset her. "I started to cry," Billie Jean said. "I stood in the locker room and cried for a long time. For a few minutes I really got scared. I wanted to run away. I wanted to do anything except walk on that court and play that match."

Billie Jean finally decided she'd worked too hard to give it all up. She conquered her nerves and Chris Evert, to win the U.S. Open title.

**Billie Jean beat sixteen-year-old Chris Evert (on the left) and went on to win the 1971 U.S. Open.**

That year turned out very well for Billie Jean. She won nineteen tournaments. She also became the first woman athlete to earn more than $100,000 in one year.

Playing tennis for money wasn't the only important thing in Billie Jean's life. Many times she gave free lessons to young people. "Kids are fun to teach," she said. "They thank you for the help you're trying to give them." Billie Jean and her husband, Larry, spent many hours helping young people play tennis. They worked to open free lesson centers throughout the country. They also worked to get college scholarships for young people who needed financial help.

Early in 1972, Billie Jean's tennis rainbow began fading. She spent many hours talking to newspaper, radio, and TV reporters. Billie Jean wanted them to cover the women's pro tennis tour. Some days she spent all her free time talking about tennis. Since Billie Jean got little rest, she felt tired and irritable.

Although Billie Jean was tired, she won many tournaments and a great deal of money. Some tennis players were jealous of Billie Jean. They also wanted to be interviewed on TV, and win tournaments and money. A few players wouldn't talk to Billie Jean in the locker room.

The long hours of practice and the jealousy of other tennis players forced Billie Jean to stop playing tennis in February, 1972. Tennis was no longer fun for her. Billie Jean and her husband, Larry, flew to Hawaii for a vacation. There, she swam and golfed, and didn't touch a racket for four weeks.

After their vacation, Billie Jean and her husband flew to San Francisco. She still didn't feel like playing tennis. Most days she went to Stinson Beach, a state park north of San Francisco. "I'd always go to the same place," she said. "There was a stump I could lean up against and watch the ocean."

"I'd just sit there. Sometimes I wrote letters. But, most of the time I'd just think. I was resting my body. But, I was resting my mind, too."

During the evenings at home, Billie Jean enjoyed reading books. *Atlas Shrugged* by Ayn Rand was one of her favorites. From that book, she learned that a deep love for something can cause both strength and weakness. She also read how success can cause envy, jealousy, and hate.

After a few weeks, Billie Jean decided to change her life style. She decided not to let other players upset her with their jealousy. "Money sure wasn't the end of my rainbow. I'd never felt money was my only reason for playing. But, I did feel I earned all the money I made. I decided to find time to relax each day."

Then, Billie Jean decided to play tournament tennis again. "I love the game too much to leave it," she said. It took her about four weeks to get back in shape. After that, she didn't lose a match for over three months.

In 1972, Billie Jean won the French Open for the first time. Then she went on to have one of her best years. She won Wimbledon and the U.S. Open! By the end of the year she had won over $100,000 again and was ranked Number One in the world.

In the 1972 finals at Wimbledon, Billie Jean smashes her way to victory over Evonne Goolagong.

Billie Jean beat Chris Evert to win her fifth Wimbledon trophy.

1973 was an even better year for Billie Jean. She won her fifth women's singles title at Wimbledon. Then, in September, she played Bobby Riggs, a famous men's tennis champion.

Billie Jean ranked that match as one of the most

important in her career. It was important because Bobby Riggs said women pros weren't worth watching. "Women shouldn't be allowed to play pro tennis," Bobby said. "They should stay home and take care of their husbands and children." Bobby said these things so more people would watch the match. However, since some fans believed Bobby, Billie Jean wanted to prove him wrong. "The match against Bobby was just as important as my 1966 Wimbledon win and my 1971 U.S. Open win over Chris Evert," she said. "In each case a defeat would've erased everything I'd done before."

Billie Jean practiced many hours for the Bobby Riggs match. She spent at least two hours every day working on just her serve. At night she lifted weights to strengthen her legs.

The day of the match, September 20, 1973, Billie Jean got up around noon. Then she started eating candy.

"Why?" sportswriters later asked.

"To build up my energy," Billie Jean said. "I ate candy all day. I also ate cheese and apples."

"What else did you do?" writers asked.

"I just lay around the hotel room. I listened to "Jesus Christ Superstar" on the radio. But, that hour before I stepped on the court was probably the toughest of my life. I worried about what would happen to women's tennis if I lost."

When Billie Jean stepped onto the tennis court,

over forty million TV viewers watched.

Billie Jean shouldn't have worried. She beat Bobby easily, 6-4, 6-3, 6-3. The victory earned her $175,000!

After accepting the winner's check, Billie Jean celebrated in a simple way. She ate ice cream with

**Billie Jean displays the trophy she won by beating Bobby Riggs.**

her husband and parents in her hotel room.

By the end of 1973, Billie Jean's total earnings topped $500,000. Some of that money came from Billie Jean's ads for tennis products. No sportswoman had ever earned as much.

George Zaharias presents Billie Jean with the Babe Didrikson Zaharias trophy as the Associated Press Female Athlete of the year for 1973. Billie Jean also won the award in 1967.

# CHAPTER 5

Early in December, 1973, Billie Jean began preparing for the 1974 tennis season. She worked out every day with several women pros. She also practiced with Tony Trabert, a Wimbledon and United States Open champion.

All that court time paid off for Billie Jean in 1974. In February she won tennis tournaments in Washington, D.C. and in Detroit, Michigan. On March 31, she defeated Chris Evert to win the National Women's Indoor Tennis Championship.

1975 was a sad year for tennis fans. In June, Billie Jean King said she would quit playing in singles tournaments after Wimbledon. "My knees hurt too much," she said.

Billie Jean retired a champion. She won the 1975 Wimbledon women's singles, defeating Evonne Goolagong. "What a way to end my career," she said. "I wanted to go out on a high. I can't get much higher than this. I think I'm the most fortunate athlete who ever lived!"

After the 1975 Wimbledon, Billie Jean earned her living working for a television network. She did reporting on tennis matches.

Billie Jean goes after a tough shot against Evonne Goolagong Cawley in the 1975 Wimbledon finals. She won the match 6-0, 6-1.

41

Since she wasn't playing tournament tennis, Billie Jean had more time to relax. "I go out to dinner and talk," she said. "I've gotten into ballet, classical music, and the arts. I'm doing things I wanted to do but never had time for."

Billie Jean's retirement didn't last long. In August, 1976, she decided to play singles matches again. She said she missed the fun of playing. In the Federation Cup, she beat Evonne Goolagong Cawley. Many tennis fans said that it was one of the best women's matches they had ever seen.

Although Billie Jean was playing excellent tennis again, her right knee still hurt her. "It felt as if someone stuck a knife under the kneecap," she said, "and lifted it." On November 9, 1976, she had her third knee operation.

After the surgery, Billie Jean began training to get back in shape. "I hated the drilling," she said. "But I know that that's what it takes for me to play well. I have to hit 250 crosscourt forehands every day and 250 down-the-lines."

It took Billie Jean until March, 1977, to get in playing shape for the women's tour. Then, she won eighteen straight matches before losing to Chris Evert, 0-6, 1-6, in the Family Circle Magazine Cup.

After the 1977 season, "World Tennis" magazine gave Billie Jean its "Achievement Award." She was honored for leadership, service to tennis, and tennis skill.

Despite a painful heel injury in 1978, Billie Jean still won many events. In 1979, after yet another operation, Billie Jean still played well. One of her most important wins was the Wimbledon doubles title with Martina Navratilova. That was Billie Jean's twentieth Wimbledon title, a record.

**Martina Navratilova and Billie Jean display their 1979 Wimbledon doubles trophy.**

After the season, Billie Jean won the Tennis Patrons' Foundation award. She was praised for "doing more for the cause of women's tennis than any person in the world."

In 1980, writers asked Billie Jean why she was still playing tournament tennis. She was thirty-six

Billie Jean won the Gunze World Tennis tournament in Toyko in 1980.

years old at the time.

"I just enjoy playing in tournaments," Billie Jean said. "I have fun, and I like to win. Tennis really turns me on. There are few thrills in life that compare with hitting a shot just right."

"Is winning tennis tournaments the most important thing for you?" writers asked.

"No," Billie Jean said, "winning isn't all that big a deal. The real joy comes from hitting that tennis ball just right. If I didn't get a pure pleasure from hitting that ball just right, I'd quit. Who in her right mind would live out of a suitcase for twenty years?"

"Has it been worth all the pain and suffering you've gone through, Billie Jean?"

"I can honestly say that it has been worthwhile. My happiness really comes from trying to reach a goal. In tennis, I can always set new goals for myself. For me, nothing is as much fun as playing tennis. I love the game."

"What if you couldn't play in tournaments anymore?"

"I honestly believe I could give up tournaments in a minute if I had to. Though I really enjoy tournaments, I'd be happy playing on a public park court two or three times a week. All I really want to do is play tennis."

And so this tennis legend keeps on slicing that ball across nets throughout the world. In September, 1980, she won a singles title in Tokyo, Japan. A

few weeks before, she and Martina Navratilova won the women's doubles at the 1980 U.S. Open.

September 16, 1980 was one of the happiest days in Billie Jean's life. On that day she was voted into the Women's Sports Hall of Fame in New York City. There, she joined such sports legends as Patty Berg and Babe Didrikson Zaharias.

What else can be said about Billie Jean King? A sports legend? Yes, her records prove it. But more importantly, she was a legend as a human being. She worked countless hours helping women gain equality in tennis.

When Billie Jean was in kindergarten, she dreamed about making her mark on the world. Her dreams came true. The marks she left on the world were freedom and equality.

## AFTERWORD

Currently Billie Jean King is living in California. She acts in commercials for television. Billie Jean also works as a broadcaster for tennis tournaments and other sporting events.

Billie Jean doesn't play as much tennis as she did when she was younger. However, she travels throughout the world giving tennis clinics.

**IF YOU ENJOYED THIS STORY, THERE ARE MORE LEGENDS TO READ ABOUT:**

PELÉ! THE SPORTS CAREER OF EDSON DO NASCIMENTO

HENRY! THE SPORTS CAREER OF HENRY AARON

TARK! THE SPORTS CAREER OF FRANCIS TARKENTON

BROWN! THE SPORTS CAREER OF JAMES BROWN

PATTY! THE SPORTS CAREER OF PATRICIA BERG

THORPE! THE SPORTS CAREER OF JAMES THORPE

ZAHARIAS! THE SPORTS CAREER OF MILDRED ZAHARIAS

SAYERS! THE SPORTS CAREER OF GALE SAYERS

CASEY! THE SPORTS CAREER OF CHARLES STENGEL

KILLY! THE SPORTS CAREER OF JEAN-CLAUDE KILLY

CHRIS! THE SPORTS CAREER OF CHRIS EVERT LLOYD

BABE! THE SPORTS CAREER OF GEORGE RUTH

KING! THE SPORTS CAREER OF BILLIE JEAN KING

WILT! THE SPORTS CAREER OF WILTON CHAMBERLAIN

ALI! THE SPORTS CAREER OF MUHAMMAD ALI